David Lyall Patrick

René Jules Dubos
Germaine Bree
Louis B. Wright

ESSAYS IN HONOR OF

David Lyall Patrick

Tucson: THE UNIVERSITY OF ARIZONA

CONTENTS

FOREWORD

DAVID LYALL PATRICK for thirty-five years was both teacher
and administrator at the University of Arizona, and was one
of the ablest and most beloved staff members. The three
lectures in this volume were presented at the University of
Arizona during the winter and spring of 1970 as a memorial
symposium honoring him. It seems appropriate to preface this
volume with a few words about those traits that made him
so respected.

Committing the elusive quality of personality to the
printed page is always a hazardous undertaking and never
more so than when the subject is a close friend. When I think
of David Patrick, his dry humor comes first to mind, and
I can imagine with what amusement he would view the
attempts to eulogize. Certainly, he would be little help, for
he never looked back; he was always concerned with what
lay ahead.

In 1934, when David applied to the University of Arizona for a vacancy in the English Department, his Stanford

teacher and colleague, Professor Hardin Craig, wrote pro-
phetically, "You will be able to use him in all sorts of ways
pertaining to the University. His advice will always be good
and he is perfectly loyal and sincere. He is humorous, pleasant,
and calm and guilty of no lost motion."

And so it turned out. The University did indeed use
him in all sorts of ways and relied unfailingly on his wisdom
and judgment. His early years at Arizona were spent on the
English faculty and then, in 1947, he became dean of the
Graduate College. He served most effectively in that post for
ten years, becoming in 1957, vice president for academic
affairs. Because of his great interest in and efforts on behalf
of the University's research program, he was persuaded to
become the first coordinator of Research, a post that was
established in 1960.

His habit of looking to the future was one of the attributes that made him so ideally suited for the new post. He
was fascinated by science and technology and eager for the
University to expand its role in these fields. As coordinator
of Research, he gave focus and direction to the efforts of perhaps a half dozen departments which had burgeoning plans
and programs and were anxious to avail themselves of the fed-
eral government's growing interest in and support of university research programs. The success of his efforts is witnessed
by the fact that when he assumed the role of coordinator, the
University was receiving considerably less than a half million
dollars in outside research support. At the time of his death,
outside funds provided more than $21 million for research
and instruction.

His effectiveness as coordinator was undoubtedly
enhanced by his ability to enjoy the confidence and friendship
of the University's scientists. They respected his judgment

and readiness with which he apprehended the essentials of highly technical and complex undertakings. When the situation required, he was their able spokesman. At the same time, he never lost sight of his first obligation and loyalty to the University and its standards. Each program or project that carried the University's endorsement for support had been first subjected to his searching scrutiny as to its soundness and suitability in terms of the University's overall objectives.

His high criteria and discerning judgment earned for the University the respect and regard of government officials who quickly came to recognize that University of Arizona proposals for support had been rigorously evaluated in advance.

David's aptitude and enthusiasm for these tasks were perhaps a bit unexpected in one whose own training and scholarship had been in the humanities.

His undergraduate work was at the University of Iowa where his father was for thirty-five years professor of philosophy. After a brief stint of high school teaching, he went to Stanford where he wrote his master's thesis in medieval literature. He then returned to Iowa to teach English and to work and study with Professor Hardin Craig on Shakespeare problems. When Professor Craig moved to Stanford, David followed him in order to complete the work he had begun. His doctoral dissertation, *The Textual History of Richard III,* was published in 1936 and reprinted in 1967. While teaching at Stanford, he continued to collaborate with Professor Craig on studies of the literature of the English renaissance. In 1934, as heretofore noted, David came to the University of Arizona as assistant professor of English.

The subsequent growth of his interest in scientific subjects was not really inconsistent. His lively intellectual curiosity ranged broadly over many fields, and he would probably

have agreed with Professor Dubos and Professor Wright that
the latter-day dichotomy between the arts and sciences ought
to be eliminated.

David's many interests found expression in his personal
life as well as in his academic career. He was an enthusiastic
devotee of sports cars and drove one himself for awhile. Always
a lover of dogs, he and his wife, Allue, were never without one.
For the last dozen or so years, two poodles, Florio and Cosette,
were their constant companions around town and the eager
greeters of callers at the home.

Thorough and painstaking in his hobbies as well as his
work, David developed professional skill as a photographer.
A favorite recreation for the Patricks was their picture-taking
trips into the hills and desert around Tucson. When university business took him out of town, his camera went along,
viewing with perceptive eye the frailties and foibles of the
human scene.

The sum of all these qualities was a personality of great
warmth and charm. Complex and acute in his intellectual
attributes, he was nevertheless outgoing and gracious. He
knew well how to put others at their ease, and this talent won
friends for the University wherever he went.

Such a man is sorely missed, and the task of expressing
the measure of his worth and our profound sense of loss is
not an easy one. The University is grateful to the Memorial
Committee for its imaginative choice of the symposium repro-
duced in these pages. The members of the committee were
Emil W. Haury, professor of anthropology, the late Francis
A. Roy, dean of Liberal Arts, and Bowen C. Dees, former
provost of the University who became president of the
Franklin Institute.

The choice of scholars who participated was also a happy one. Professor Germaine Bree, of the University of Wisconsin's Institute for Research in the Humanities, analyzes with great skill the role of the poet in today's fragmented world. Professor René Dubos of Rockefeller University, sees an overriding need for science and the humanities to join forces in assisting man in his search for an understanding of his own place in the order of things. And Louis B. Wright, historian and former director of the Folger Shakespeare Library, finds lessons for our time in the disciplined learning of the renaissance and in the commingling of science and humanism in that period.

The University of Arizona is pleased to present this distinguished collection of papers in book form, thus making them available to an even wider audience than those that were privileged to attend the David Lyall Patrick Memorial Symposium.

RICHARD A. HARVILL
President

CIVILIZING TECHNOLOGY

RENÉ JULES DUBOS, humanist author and biographer of science and scientists, has written several distinguished books for both scholars and the lay reader on topics relating to microbiology, bacteriology, and psychophysiology. Recipient of numerous scientific awards and honorary degrees from research institutions in Europe and the United States, he joined the faculty of Rockefeller University in 1957, having previously served as professor of pathology and tropical medicine at Harvard Medical School. Among his published works best known to the general public are *Man and Society, The Mirage of Health, The Dreams of Reason, Pasteur and Modern Medicine, The Unseen World, The Torch of Life, Health and Disease,* and *Man Adapting.*

CIVILIZING TECHNOLOGY

René Jules Dubos

IN OUR TROUBLED TIMES, some reassurance may be found in the fact that the word *civilization* was used for the first time during a period even more troubled than ours. Shortly before the American and French Revolutions, the Marquis de Mirabeau published an essay that he entitled "L'Amy des Femmes ou Traité de la Civilisation." In it, he gave credit to women for most of the improvements that he regarded essential to what he called a civilized life. But he used the new word *civilization* in a much more restricted sense than is the usual practice. For Mirabeau, and for most of the philosophers of the Enlightenment, civilization referred to gentle ways of life, humane laws, limitations on war, a high level of purpose and conduct.

The Industrial Revolution soon generated a view of civilized life far different from that held during the eighteenth century. Throughout the nineteenth century, new technological developments brought about an immense increase in wealth, in Europe first and then in the United States. The success of Western civilization was measured by the production of food and manufactured articles, rather than by the quality of human relationships. Until recently, indeed, it was considered justifiable to identify industrial civilization with the welfare of mankind because technological advances had done so much during the late nineteenth and early twentieth centuries to make human life more comfortable, healthier, longer, and richer in experience.

Scientific technology was on the whole the servant of man during the first phases of the Industrial Revolution. But its human orientation has decreased during the few decades past to such an extent that some of its manifestations now threaten the welfare of mankind. This trend was clearly recognized by Henry Adams in the chapter of his *Education* entitled "The Dynamo and the Virgin."

Watching the displays in the Galerie des Machines at the 1900 Paris World's Fair, Adams became convinced that mechanical forces had now replaced spiritual and emotional motivation in the governance of human affairs.

The view of social change that Henry Adams symbolized by the substitution of the Dynamo for the Virgin was stated more directly and bluntly in the guidebook of the 1933 Chicago World's Fair. The fair celebrated the "Century of Progress" that had created the wealth of Chicago since the birth of the city in 1833, and that was identified with the development of scientific technology. As stated in the guidebook of the fair:

"Science discovers, genius invents, industry applies, and *man adapts himself to, or is molded by,* new things . . . Individuals, groups, entire races of *men fall into step* with . . . science and industry." [Italics mine]

A large sculptural group in the Hall of Science at the

fair went even further than the text of the guidebook in conveying the thought that machines had become more powerful than the human spirit. The sculpture showed a man and a woman with hands outstretched as if in fear of ignorance; between them stood a huge angular robot nearly twice their size bending low over them, with an angular metallic arm thrown reassuringly around each. Technology protecting and guiding mankind was indeed the theme of the fair.

Since the organizers of the Chicago fair took it for granted that everything developed by scientific technology was good for man, they found it natural to use as a heading in their guidebook:

Science Finds
Industry Applies
Man Conforms

The phrase "Man Conforms" had sinister implications for the welfare of mankind, even in 1933. It implied that man must conform to the environment created by industry, instead of using science and technology to develop conditions really suited to fundamental human needs. These implications, however, did not become widely recognized until the mid-century, when the mounting roster of environmental problems had made it obvious to all that the technological way of life is not necessarily conducive to health and happiness.

The beginning of a movement against the view that man must "conform" to the dictates of technology can be seen in the popular success of the Environmental Teach-In on Earth Day, April, 1970. Some aspects of contemporary youth culture also express a rejection of this view. More importantly, they constitute an attempt to recapture essential human values which are rapidly disappearing from the technological world.

Interest in bright colors, in exotic and interesting smells, in
gay sounds as from the tinkling of bells, in love and tribal life,
in the practice of handicrafts and in a return to nature — all
these expressions of the contemporary youth culture at its best
correspond to values that technological civilization is destroy-
ing or at the very least ignoring. Society must give an important place to these values because they are as essential to
health and happiness as is the supply of pure air, pure water,
and pure food.

Rejection of the matter-oriented, almost antihuman value
system which is presently dominating Western civilization is
fortunately occurring at a time when physical, ecological, and
demographic forces inevitably will compel a restructuring of
social and technological organization. Whether we want it
or not, the phase of quantitative growth which has prevailed
during the nineteenth and twentieth centuries must soon come
to an end. Modern industrial societies can survive only if they
make *quality* of life, rather than *quantity* of production, the
criterion of their success.

Here are a few of the reasons, dogmatically stated, which
lead me to believe that the phase of quantitative growth of our
society will soon come to an end:

1. World population will stop growing and may even
decrease under the pressure of different forces. In some parts
of the world, this will happen as a result of food shortages;
biological disasters such as mass disease and mass poisoning
are likely to occur in other areas; willful control of birthrates
will be achieved in a few countries.

2. The amount of energy used for industrial and domestic
purposes will eventually reach a plateau — even if new kinds
of low-cost fuels become available and if the production of
"clean" nuclear energy becomes technologically possible. The

limitation will come not from shortage of energy sources, but from the fact that the injection of excessive amounts of energy into natural systems inevitably disturbs their operations and commonly leads to ecological disasters. Thermal pollution is the best understood of these forms of ecological threat. The more general statement, however, is that all forms of power pollute.

3. The quantity of things produced by technology will also reach a plateau, because of shortages in certain natural resources and because environmental pollution will reach unbearable levels. The present accumulation of solid wastes — chemical and organic — is a portent of worse things to come.

The population of the United States is increasing at a rate of approximately 1 percent a year. In contrast, the production of electric energy and the accumulation of wastes are increasing at the rate of 9 percent a year — which means that they will double in less than eight years. In view of these facts, environmental degradation and loss in the quality of life would continue to accelerate very rapidly in the United States even if we were to succeed in achieving Zero Population Growth. The impact of technology therefore constitutes a more immediate threat than the population bomb and far more destructive, because many of its effects will be irreversible.

All ecological systems, whether man-made or natural, must in the long run achieve a state of equilibrium and be self-regenerating with regard to both energy and materials. The ecology of highly industrialized nations has been in a state of disequilibrium for several decades. Furthermore, ecological instability is increasing at a rate so accelerated that disasters are inevitable if the trend continues. We cannot afford to delay much longer the development of a nearly

"closed" system in which materials will retain their value
throughout the system by being recycled instead of being dis-
carded as pollutants.

The ecological constraints on population and technological growth will inevitably lead to social and economic systems
different from the ones in which we have been living. In fact,
all this was foreseen more than a century ago by John Stuart
Mill who coined the phrase "stationary state," to denote a
stage of Western civilization in which further *quantitative*
growth would no longer be possible. Even though events will
certainly validate John Stuart Mill's conclusions, the adjec-
tive "stationary" that he uses to define the forthcoming phase
is unfortunate, because it seems to imply a complete end to
change. The phase "steady state" is more compatible with a
dynamic equilibrium and continued *qualitative* change.

The "steady state" formula is so different from the philosophy of endless quantitative growth, which has governed
Western civilization during the nineteenth and twentieth
centuries, that it may cause public alarm. Many persons will
mistakenly assume that the world is entering a period of stag-
nation, leading eventually to decadence. Yet, a steady state
can be favorable to creative change. In fact, change within a
closed system will probably offer intellectual possibilities much
more challenging than those offered by rampant growth of the
kind that prevails at present. For example, it would demand
of General Motors, or any large corporation, a higher degree
of inventiveness, initiative, and social concern to design and
produce means of transport really suited to American life,
rather than to continue the present practice of producing
monotonously, boringly, destructively bigger, flashier, and
more and more costly automobiles.

Shifting emphasis from an increase in the quantity of
production to an improvement in the quality of life will inevit-

ably generate new kinds of social, intellectual, and scientific problems. To illustrate, we need mention only a few problems arising from the ecological constraints on the growth of the world population and on the production of energy and goods:

— the drastic limitation of family size will probably create social, psychological, physiological, and perhaps even genetic disturbances concerning which little, if anything, is known.

— the distribution and utilization of energy under controlled conditions will require sophisticated knowledge of regional and global ecology.

— entirely new technologies, and therefore new kinds of scientific knowledge, will have to be developed to minimize pollution and to recycle natural resources.

The steady state will thus compel a reorientation of the scientific, technologic, and economic enterprise. Indeed, it may generate a social renaissance. But this will not happen without a conscious and probably painful effort from the academic and business community.

Paradoxical as it may seem, most of the determinants of the quality of life have their origin deep in the evolutionary past. It is true of course that man's powers for social adaptability have enabled him to survive, multiply, and function under conditions very different from the ones under which he evolved, but this does not mean that his nature has changed. Wherever modern man lives and whatever he does, his fundamental characteristics remain much the same as they were during the Stone Age. His biological needs, emotional urges, and even many of his aspirations are still very similar to those of the paleolithic hunter and the neolithic farmer.

All aspects of human life are so conditioned by the past that the frontiers of social and technological developments should be determined, not by availability of natural resources or scientific know-how, but by the biological limitations and potentialities of man which are elements in the genetic code he inherited from his Stone Age ancestors. To be viable, or at least compatible with human welfare, social and technological innovations must be fitted to the needs, limitations, potentialities, and aspirations of the man of flesh and bone. It is this criterion which provides the most intimate points of contact between the humanities and the sciences, as well as with religious ideals.

All great civilizations have begun with a religious impetus which provided man with a sense of his relation to the cosmos and with images of the future, and thus helped him to contest reality and create history.

A religious attitude, governing the formulation of ends and the creation of history, naturally implies value judgments and therefore is highly personal or at least culture bound. There are some values, however, which are almost universal because they are intimately bound to man's fundamental nature. As a result they are relevant to humanistic and scientific studies, and can lead to action programs meaningful for all human beings.

Every aspect of our life is conditioned by the stimuli we receive from the physical, biological, and social environment. Beyond that, there is much more to the earth than the pleasure it gives our senses. This blue planet is responsible for our very nature because human beings are shaped, biologically and mentally, by the environment in which they develop. The earth is our mother not only because of nurturing us now, but even more because our biological and mental being has emerged from the earth during evolutionary times and is constantly maintained and shaped by its influence throughout our present existence. We could not long remain true human beings if we were to settle on the moon or on Mars, and we shall progressively lose our humanness if we continue to destroy the unique qualities of the earth by pouring filth into the atmosphere, befouling the soil, lakes, and rivers, disfiguring the landscapes with junkpiles. Man is of the earth, earthy. The quality of his life is inextricably interwoven with the quality of the earth and of the life it harbors.

The enchanting diversity of the earth comes from the multiplicity of its living forms, each fitted to a particular place and contributing to its genius. Although modern man has placed himself somewhat outside natural systems, he can and should play a creative role in their quality by substituting for the contemporary doctrines of conquest and exploitation a philosophy of conscious design based on ecological knowledge. There would thus emerge a scientific basis for a theology of the earth.

Religious attitudes, even though derived from a theology of the earth based on concrete biological values, must always express themselves through cultural forms, and in turn they affect the evolution of the culture.

Cultural forms imply creative acts through which the community as a whole, or individual persons, impose esthetic and social design on men, surroundings, and events. To be viable, however, the patterns thus created must be compatible with the constraints inherent in man's nature, and in the characteristics of the climate and the land. Cultural design must be governed by ecological considerations.

The fundamental and unchangeable needs of man are easier to understand when it is realized that the cradle of *Homo sapiens* was on the pleasant plateaus of East Africa. A million years ago, the human species emerged in a land of hills and valleys, of springs and streams, of varied woodland, shrubs and herbs. Its early homes were probably alluvial plains and rock shelters in cliffs. The climate was subtropical, with alternating rainy and dry seasons and with growing and resting periods of vegetation. All in all, this was a type of country and of climate that most people still associate with pleasant living conditions. In fact, most human beings are best adapted to the Riviera or California-like conditions that probably fostered the emergence of the human species.

Pastoral life is obviously associated with some of the most pleasant memories of mankind; an image of it is presented in the Biblical paradise. Many dominant themes of classical mythology unfold in pastoral landscapes with a subtropical climate. Countless bucolic paintings have depicted pastures shaded with beautiful trees under which youths engage in the games of love, while shepherds tend grazing animals.

Unfortunately, few are the parts of the parts of the world which now provide conditions similar to the park-like landscape symbolized by the name Arcadia and idealized for example in Giorgione's famous painting "Concert Champetre." As a substitute, men have tried for scores of centuries to duplicate in their houses the climatic conditions of the semitropical zone in which the human species emerged. In his book *The Tropical Life of the Eskimos,* the explorer V. Stefansson claimed that, wrapped in their parkas and sheltered within their igloos, even Eskimos manage to live much of the time in a very warm environment despite the Arctic cold. Wherever they can, men create near their homes parks and gardens which remind them of pastoral scenes.

The development of air-conditioning techniques has now made it possible to create artificially a semitropical environment everywhere on earth, and even in space capsules. But this does not mean that maintaining the temperature of our dwellings and offices at a constant level of 72°-75° F is necessarily the formula best suited to human beings, if we remember that primitive man was exposed to marked daily and seasonal fluctuations throughout his evolutionary development. Since man has not changed biologically, one may postulate that programming seasonal and diurnal fluctuations into air-conditioning systems might have desirable physiological effects.

So many behavioral traits have been inherited from our Stone Age ancestors that the best relic of early man is modern man. Paleolithic hunters, and probably for a long time neolithic farmers, lived in small bands having only rare and limited contacts with other groups. Such social conditions must have favored the development of a sense of territoriality and also some form of loyalty to the few members of the band. These attitudes are still reflected in our behavior. The word *stranger* has unpleasant connotations in all languages, and the range of meaningful, close relationships is in general limited to a small number of persons even in large urban centers.

Even the form of social conflicts is conditioned by the distant past. In animal populations and in very primitive human societies, competition between groups is rarely destructive, because it is resolved through ritualized conflicts that rarely result in mortal wounds. In the ritualized conflict, one of the antagonists accepts defeat and leaves the field to the opponent appearing to be the strongest. Jousting between medieval knights and other such historical practices may have been human forms of ritualized conflict. Optimists suggest that the space race between the United States and the Soviet Union might be regarded as a form of ritualized conflict and perhaps even serve as a substitute for war.

Man's distant past also affects his reaction to crowding. From time immemorial, human beings have been tolerant of high population density. The neolithic settlements, the medieval towns, the Pueblo villages of the Rio Grande, had small populations in comparison with our cities, but their areas were so much smaller that their population density was very high. Manhattan has a lower population density than European or Asian cities of the past and even of the present.

More important than the population density of a given area is the origin of its inhabitants. Until recent times, large and small cities consisted in very large part of people who, although belonging to different social groups, were familiar with each other because of the integrated activities of daily life. This experience gave them the opportunity to develop protective social mechanisms which helped in reducing violent social conflict. In our times, however, the great mobility of all classes of people has caused massive and sudden admixtures of population especially in American cities. Our evolutionary past has not prepared us for rapid changes in population structure. Whatever the color of his skin, the stranger is still a potential enemy. The hostility to him derives in large part from the apprehension he engenders.

Even when man has become an urbane city dweller, the paleolithic bull which survives in his inner self still paws the earth whenever anything unexpected or threatening appears on the social scene. Our body and mind still respond to environmental stimuli as did that of our paleolithic ancestors — except that the response now rarely takes an actual physical form; hence, many of the nervous tensions in modern life.

The survival of needs that have their origin in the distant past manifests itself in our daily life. We build wood fires in steam-heated city apartments; we keep plants and animals around us as if to maintain direct contact with our own origins; we travel long and far on weekends to recapture some aspect of the wilderness from which our ancestors emerged centuries ago. When we can afford it, we go back to hunting, first using guns, then bows and arrows; we may come to use spears armed with points fashioned from stones with our own hands — not out of necessity, but as a symbol of return to the Stone Age.

In the preceding pages, I have deliberately discussed as a totality the problems relating to religion, the arts, technology, and a host of other theoretical and practical subjects. My purpose was to illustrate and emphasize that all aspects of life can be considered from both the humanistic and scientific point of view. On the other hand, there is no doubt that profound differences exist between these two approaches to understanding and action.

Humanists tend to perceive the world of reality or of imagination as an integrated whole. They apprehend and express the human condition by observing and describing in a holistic way the experiential manifestation of man's interplay with his total environment. In contrast, men trained in the natural or social sciences always analyze existing situations or possibilities by breaking them up into their component parts. Their approach is to consider separately all the fragments of experience and their goal is to discover which components of the system can be manipulated successfully and usefully. As a result, scientists are prone to fractionate reality into manageable subsystems and to devise artificial models which they can understand and control. Such models lack the warmth of reality but precise knowledge of them guides and facilitates the manipulation of human problems.

Scientists have often been more interested in their models than in reality, more concerned with abstract technological utopias than with the unchangeable needs of man's nature, which are the expression of the living past. But these are limitations of science as it is practiced today rather than of science as an intellectual discipline. Relating science to human needs will simply require the design of more complex models, incorporating more and more components of the human condition and of the ecological systems in which man functions. It is not man which must conform to technology, but technology which must be made to conform to the human condition.

The most significant contact between the humanities and the sciences will eventually take place at a level much deeper than technological applications and will reach into man's subconscious apprehension of reality. It will be concerned with man's understanding of his place in the cosmic order of things and may help him to recover some of his primitive ability to apprehend creation in a holistic manner.

The words of wisdom and the mystic experiences that have come to us from very ancient cultures had their origin in man's direct and intimate contact with the world of reality. Most of us, in the technological world, have unfortunately lost the power to establish contact with the natural forces that have shaped man's senses and brain in the course of his evolutionary development.

By learning to recapture once more the direct experience of reality, through the humanistic approach, and searching for fundamental patterns through the abstractions of science, we may finally discover the nature of our real being as part of the order from which we emerged.

This discovery of the self and of our organic relation to nature may have been what T. S. Eliot had in mind when he wrote the following words — which express my own attitude toward science and the humanities:

> We shall not cease from exploration
> And the end of all our exploring
> Will be to arrive where we started
> And know the place for the first time.

LITERATURE TODAY

GERMAINE BREE, educator and humanistic scholar, has written extensively in the fields of literary history and criticism, focusing on Marcel Proust, and the contemporary fiction of Albert Camus and other literati of modern France. An authority on French language and literature, she has served on the National Committee for French Government Awards, and in the United States as an advisory board member of the American Council of Learned Societies. She headed the Department of Romance Languages at New York University until 1958 when she joined the University of Wisconsin faculty as chairman of the Department of Romance Languages and Russian, and professor in the Institute for Research in the Humanities. Her published volumes include *Camus*; *Proust*; *An Age of Fiction*; *Voix d'aujourd'hui*; and *The World of Marcel Proust*.

LITERATURE TODAY

Germaine Bree

NOT TOO LONG AGO, students at the University of Wisconsin organized a week of lectures on the state of our environment. Each one of the experts called upon to speak had his very real concern: the population explosion; water, air, soil, food, DDT, nuclear pollution; waste. The lectures started with an objective appraisal of the situation, then leaped to the prophetic: as a species we were on the way out. They gave us ten or perhaps twenty years — unless . . . . The prescriptions were diverse, urgent and contradictory, and it was clear that they could hardly be implemented within the span of time allotted. Toward the end of the week a group of students engaged in the ritual orgy of "trashing." True it was probably mere coincidence; but it is true too that when people feel impotent in the face of disaster they tend to react by perpetrating violence.

At the end of the week three professors representing the Humanities — philosophy, history and literature — were called upon to conclude the debate and pronounce on the chances and modes of man's survival. We were baffled. For we had no

answers as Humanists; we could speak only in terms of our
subjective beliefs and common sense. Being closer than the
students to our own private apocalypse, we could only say that
yes, indeed, we thought humanity would survive. But I, for
example, in the name of literature, could not truthfully say
that it would help matters if literature were more vividly
taught in schools and colleges and if more people read and
wrote literary works.

If I recall this episode typical of many such today with the
same attendant frustrations, it is because it illustrates the kind
of misunderstanding which haunts the attempts of writers,
readers and teachers to define with some degree of pertinency
the function in our contemporary society of that particular
human activity — the creation of literature. I shall use the
word here in the more special sense as referring to those works
that belong to the sphere of "belles-lettres" and shall not
attempt further to define it, for that would involve unlimited
debate. We are dealing with an academic discipline whose
realm is not strictly defined, for what makes a text "literary" is
open to question, but the query nonetheless is central to our
educational edifice. What, some of our students are now ask-
ing, is the use of Shakespeare, for example, when we confront
the dereliction of the ghetto? In practical terms the answer is
"none." It is a fact that literature does not deal in immediate
practical solutions. Then the question arises: in a time of
urgent social problems why fiddle while Detroit burns? or
while millions of human beings suffer hunger?

From time immemorial, the poet — taking the word in its
broadest sense — and the nature of his activity have been
topics of speculation; the poet has always been with us.
Periodically — as in France, for instance, in the last half-

century — the question arises "What is literature?" "Why write?" "For whom does one write?" It was Sartre who again raised these questions with great rhetorical urgency immediately after World War II. These questions are among our preoccupations today. Writers, philosophers, critics, educators join in the debate and, it seems, never fully agree as to the answer. Now, as in the past, no answer seems definitive. In learned journals and popular magazines time-honored definitions are proposed, and writers themselves come forth with conflicting claims. We are living in a time when the literary experience is being newly scrutinized, from every angle — the writer's, the reader's, the critic's, the educator's, the psychologist's, the sociologist's, the philosopher's. But then so is our entire outlook on what the existentialist philosophers like to call our "human reality." The connection is not accidental.

Our students will challenge most of the time-honored justifications of literature: that it is a central part of our cultural heritage; that it is a source of inner enrichment and wisdom, expanding our awareness, refining our sensibilities; that it is in essence a celebration of life, of man's presence in and to the world; and one of the noblest repositories of men's dreams, insights and understanding; and that, consequently, it must be passed on from generation to generation giving the succeeding generations a sense of the values inherent in the human enterprise. They challenge also our assumption that like all the other arts literature is indispensable to our post-Nietzschean age in which for many people "God is dead" and for whom there is no reality beyond this earth, a recurrent theme in contemporary thought.

We also know from experience that a high level of literary culture has not proved incompatible in our time — or in any

time — with a fine capacity for organized brutality. The Nazi
example, though the most dramatic, is unfortunately not the
only example we might consider. Marx, besides, has suggested
to us that writers are socially "conditioned" and may unknow-
ingly wear the same blinders as their contemporaries, exhibit
the same mental bounds. So that we may wonder to what
extent and in what sense literature in fact *informs* us. In the
past, as sometimes still in the present, large claims have been
put forward with messianic fervor and have not seemed
entirely convincing. There was the surrealistic claim that if
literature were what it should be, it could "transform" life;
the Marxist-Hegelian claim that its function is to collaborate
with history in the necessary and inevitable movement of
human society through time; the liberal belief that it is the
highest manifestation of a culture, carefully to be nurtured;
and in contrast that flat assertion of a French poet — Mal-
herbe — in the seventeenth century that a writer is of no more
use to the state than a bowler — a point of view which we
seem uneasily and unconvincingly to be struggling to disprove.

We feel, nonetheless, consternation, and sometimes a
sense of suffocation as books proliferate, and we confront, in
paperback, the acres of "bad, good, indifferent, eccentric and
stuffy works" of literature that have come down to us through
the centuries and from all across the earth. As they rush
through academic reading lists, students acquire the feeling
that they are caught in a treadmill of words and want to get
out of it and live. Literature then may appear to them in a
simple way as antithetical to life: and that too is a literary
theme in itself. But, until the last quarter of a century we
had assumed that if we as individual subjects are not here to
stay, others would necessarily come after us to pursue the
human venture where we left off, that there would be a con-
tinuity in the development of our civilization. We were no

longer too sure of what that individual "I" represented. Freud had split it at least into three — the Ego, the Id and the Super-ego; Marx had suggested that we were merely the products of economic forces; philosophers such as Sartre taught us that we are nothing but the sum of our acts; others such as Nietzsche and Wittgenstein had turned the spotlight on our language. We are living in the age of structural linguistics which proves to us that language, independently of our conscious will, controls our manner of being and creates our way of looking at the world — biological structures, social structures, linguistic structures, literary structures. Non-experts are wary today of making any statements describing human beings and their activities. The French novelist Nathalie Sarraute claims that today's writer lives in the "age of suspicion" in regard to his craft. We might prefer to call it the age of questioning.

In the meantime Professor McLuhan has proclaimed in a widely-circulated book that "the book" is on its way out, at least in the form we know, displaced by the electronic audio-visual media and ephemeral psychodelic environmental forms of art. We had realized, of course, that we were living in a period of unusually fast change and witnessing the destruction — gradual or abrupt — of many social and esthetic assumptions and traditions. Rightly sometimes, though rashly at other times, the young men and women around us were intimating that they did not intend to let us continue with staid placidity producing well-worn answers to their questions. "How can you put on yesterday's clothes?" the Surrealists already had queried rather more forcibly than avant-garde groups before them.

In the modern world, environmental experts, in their anxiety over the predicaments they had diagnosed, had created an unprecedented situation for us: they were cutting us off

from the continuum of time. Unprecedented is not quite the
right term; human beings, periodically, have been haunted by
the specter of the end of the world. But this "sense of an
ending" was developing in the context of the *scientific* study
of phenomena — not religious, or visionary prediction — and
thereby was unprecedented in its impact. In his articles Professor René Dubos has spoken of what may happen to human
beings when changes in their outer and inner environment
are too abrupt. And the two are not unrelated. What we tend
to forget in our debates is the *inner* environment, the inner
ambiance to which the debates are related and the inner disturbances they engender. Since Hiroshima that "sense of an
ending" has been with us and we suffer a latent unease born
of the individual's impatience with a society that spells out the
danger and yet apparently will not change, and so, in the
opinion of some, must be radically rejected and smashed.

To speak of literature in this perspective seems inappro-
priate: a poem, a novel — on the same scale of values, all
"irrelevant," barring some magic formula — can hardly com-
pete against the fascination, the power over the imagination
of such an anticipation. If the Apocalypse is near, speech of
any kind would appear as nothing but senseless chatter, a
noisy form of silence.

Senseless chatter and silence indeed have furnished the
content, if not the substance of some recent literature: of the
early Ionesco plays, and increasingly, the work of Beckett.
Yet, paradoxically, in the literary transmutation, the sense-
lessness acquires meaning and the silence becomes communication. With his sardonic sense of humor Beckett has recently
pushed his experiments with minimal expressions to its limits:
the vague glimpse of a medley of bodies, and a wail. Recently
a French scholar and psychiatrist, Michel Foucault, has suggested that madness occurs when a person is placed in condi-

tions such that, paralyzed by the sense of his finitude, he is no longer able to grasp any image of himself as engaged in the "signifying" (meaningful) human activities: language, work and living; overwhelmed by the "non-sense" of his being, he then "throws in the towel." As the activities of Ionesco and Beckett suggest, the writer is the man who, as long as he writes, cannot "throw in the towel." By the very fact that he is giving some shape or form to the words he gathers he is engaged in a "signifying" activity. To write is to wager against the Apocalypse. This of course could probably be argued as holding true of all art. I shall now try to approach the topic of literature proper from another point of view.

In an issue of the *New York Review of Books* (April 9, 1970) Kenneth Koch of Columbia University tells of his experimental class in New York City the purpose of which was to teach fourth and fifth graders to write poetry. The article is entitled *Wishes, Lies and Dreams,* a Freudian title. Koch describes his method as follows: "I asked the class to write a poem together, everybody contributing one line . . . Everyone was to write the line on a sheet of paper and turn it in . . . I suggested we make some rules about what should be in every line . . . it would help to give the final poem unity . . . I gave an example putting a color in every line." The poem was to be an "I wish" poem. "We ended up with the regulation that every line should contain a color, a comic-strip character, and a city or country." The method as you see recalls certain surrealistic experiments. The lines were shuffled; the title chosen by the children was "Feelings at P.S. 61." This is what came out:

> *I wish I was Dick Tracy in a black suit in England*
> *I wish I were a Supergirl with a red cape; the city of*
>   *Mexico is where I live*

> *I wish that I were Veronica in South America. I*
> *wish that I could see the blue sky . . . and so on.*

The children, Mr. Koch tells us, were enormously excited first
by writing the lines, then even more by hearing them read
as a poem. They were, he says "talking, waving, blushing,
laughing and bouncing up and down." Mr. Koch then had
each child write his own "wish poem."

> *I wish I could leap high into the air and land softly*
> *on my toes*
> *I wish I could dance in every country in the world . . . .*

And he read the best of these to the primary grades. "Within
a few moments," he writes "first a few students then the whole
class was shouting 'Yeah!' at the top of their lungs after every
wish, that is after every line of every poem." They too wanted
to write and they did.

The environment was drab, but the children were com-
pletely uninhibited by it, tremendously happy and totally
absorbed in their activity. What they had discovered, one
surmises, was their power over and freedom in language, their
ability to take the words and sensations and feelings of everyday living and give them a new kind of presence, new yet
specific and recognizable. And each wish of each separate
child was recognized and hailed by them all.

In a recent book entitled *The Seamless Web* (Braziller,
New York, 1970), the poet and critic Stanley Burnshaw
examines the artist's — more specifically the poet's — activity,
in the light both of the psychophysiology of which Professor
Dubos is an exponent and of linguistics. Poetry, he claims

begins and ends with the body. He describes the creative process in terms of the physical processes described by contemporary biology whereby the "human creature" responds to the world as a total organism in order to maintain the equilibrium that allows it to survive in its environment. The "human creature" is the talking creature and still — pace McLuhan — in some reaches of our society the writing creature. Literature in its *broadest* sense Mr. Burnshaw sees as linked to the needs of the total organism and as such he defines it as "the joint creation of man and his universe." It is one of the means we have of creating the equilibrium between and the merging of man and world that can come into being through language. In our complex society, he suggests, as others also have suggested, this equilibrium is reached by the controlled expression — through pattern, rhythm, tempo, and all forms of stylization — of those organic impulses driven into obscurity by the abstract computer-like thought processes predominant in the organization of a high civilization. Literary creation in those terms is a necessary activity, a "life-sustaining" activity, a verbal "unburdening" that establishes a truce in our complicated conflict-ridden lives. For Burnshaw, then, writing and reading in the deepest sense are "natural" activities through which we re-establish our often fragile sense of existing as a part of what he calls "the seamless web of the world." Though I am not arguing that the lines written at P.S. 16 constitute "high" literature, they do in many ways corroborate Mr. Burnshaw's description of his much more conscious activity: the "unburdening," the link established between the I and the outer world, the joy in the pattern which is a sign of control.

What I am suggesting then is that what we question and argue about when we talk of literature is not so much the

fact of the literary experience as the *manner* in which we
should look at it and talk about it. The writer himself when
he wants to communicate his experience often reaches out to
the ideas and knowledge that are current in his society. Where
some will settle for "genius," to explain what they do, others
will speak of the unconscious self, and Mr. Burnshaw notes
that "language speaks me." But all are speaking of the literary
venture as a discovery of something "other" than the everyday
modes of speech. It is easy to see how aptly Mr. Koch worked,
somewhat as many modern artists work, by proposing to his
class an arbitrary but single structure. One element was the
subjective "I wish" that liberated the children from the restric-
tive context of the immediate reality around them and let
them loose in a whole inner world of words, images and
memory, in which they felt free and excited by what they
discovered. He then directed their attention to random group-
ings of things — color, place, names of imaginary but familiar
figures. And so he had made heterogeneous fragmented things
hang together; he had made them show themselves in unexpected ways, never the same things, never in the same way
for two children.

The principle of unification proposed was not externally
formal but it allowed the children to create forms while giving
them an escape from learned, expected associations. Part of
the children's pleasure (what poet was it who said that we
need to "redeem" pleasure?) certainly was due to their recognition of the recurrent design and of the inexhaustible diversity
of the mutations that they could create within it. In an unso-
phisticated way they were at the heart of the literary experience. In a wholly unconscious manner they were experiencing
what, in their different theoretic approaches, some of our
"structuralists" are suggesting — whether in anthropology,

psychology, art or linguistics — that a language is a symbolic system that "makes sense" because, beneath the surface of the words, there is an underlying structure that makes it possible to communicate variants and so to introduce modes of individual feelings and experience — the modes of feeling of a particular concrete physical being, in a particular setting, a particular society and time.

"Our man-made environment," writes an environmentalist, "is the most significant creation of all time in that it has the most immediate effect on men's lives and souls." And yet, he continues, "the traditional humanistic education provides little guidance for anyone" who wants to "evaluate the complex changing environment." He has, I fear, forgotten the whole vast edifice of the arts and singularly of literature which is a privileged domain of speech. For to some extent, no literature, when we become familiar with its patterns of language, remains foreign to us. It is itself an environment, built in time, a collective enterprise in that sense, something abiding and that can be present to us, if not actually in its entirety, at least virtually so. And it transmits our multiple and complex relations with the world outside us — our "wishes, lies, and dreams" as well as our observations and experiences and what we make of them.

Mr. Koch's experiment with the fourth and fifth graders in New York City suggests that the impulse to create our own patterns of language from within the common language we speak is, as Stanley Burnshaw says, basic; and, as Burnshaw also advances, it is possibly the only way we have of living fully one of our potentialities. All of us will not realize that particular way; but all of us can recognize it in its realization. Mr. Koch gave a simple pattern to the children to work on. The serious writer must of course find his own patterns that

bridge as best they may the gap between his personal relation
to the world and the general or more abstract views given him
by his culture and latent in his language. The gap between the
two in our contemporary world has seemed wide. We lack an
overall and explicit general view of our own being even when
we are able to grasp the representations of biology, physics,
astronomy, and so on. We are people of many worlds, new
worlds with new perspectives. Hence the restlessness in all
the arts, the impulse toward what a critic has called "decrea-
tion," the artist's refusal of familiar, traditional forms. And in
many people this break with the past engenders a sense of
panic and hostility. With increasing rapidity artists establish
and tear down one new pattern after another. The arts of our
time — literature among them — are described in such terms
as randomness, multiplicity of patterning, afocality, frag-
mentation, often seeming to the layman to be animated by
what Morse Peckham has called "a rage for chaos." Avant-
garde experiments are picked up, avidly discussed, theorized,
and buried under those that follow. It is not that the *process*
is new. The dialectic of destruction and creation is familiar,
but its disconcerting pace is new and the sense that it is often
instigated from outside, by the needs of the reviews and journals which must have something "newsworthy" to report.
Many young Americans now look upon our traditional respect
for art as nothing more than a clever "put-on," a way to sell
on the market another "bourgeois" commodity.

It is never easy to see clearly what is actually taking place
in literature around us. We know how easily we can our-
selves distinguish the order we want to see, and we know also
that a great deal of insignificant writing does get published.
Moreover no one can speak adequately of literature in general.

A literary work has to be present to us in its particularity, before we can say anything pertinent about it.

I was asked to consider whether I thought that contemporary literature, as is sometimes alleged, had failed to express in a significant way the concerns of our time. It is true of course that a predominant trend in contemporary literature surfaced with the Dadaist proclamation of their purpose to destroy literature along with all the manifestations of our culture. Much of our literature does have a disturbing aura of "cruelty" in the sense connoted by Antonin Artaud in the thirties when he called for a "theater of cruelty." It deliberately aims at shocking our sensibility. But when we look more closely at our recent literature — the French in particular since that is where my own interests specifically center — we see other trends also. There is, for instance, a determined effort to move language out of abstract verbal patterns into a confrontation with the concrete world of bodies and objects. This is no doubt a perilous statement to make in the era of abstract art. But writers are struggling, if I may borrow the expression from an as yet unpublished work by Sanford Ames, to "put our minds back in our bodies and our bodies back in the world." The surrealist revolt in one of its aspects proclaimed the immediate presence of the human being as a whole person to the world and proposed that we renew the way in which we inhabit our world.

> *Nothing can upset the order of light*
> *Where I am only myself*
> *And what I love*
> *And on the table*
> *This jug full of water and the bread of rest.**

---

* Paul Eluard quoted by Mary Ann Caws in *The Poetry of Dada and Surrealism*, Princeton University Press, 1970, p. 24.

This insistence on the immediate and the specific is at the heart of Camus's work which is modern in its sensibility while its forms evolve within the mainstream of French literary tradition; and that has been most certainly a factor in its appeal. The same insistence on the immediate and specific is the facet of the Surrealists' venture which is still very much with us, whereas in contrast writers on the whole have tended to abandon the great surrealist ambition to solve our metaphysical problems.

A quite differently inspired writer such as the poet, Ponge, whose work seems at the opposite pole from the Surrealists', has the same fascination with regard to objects. He makes a careful and slow approach to the most familiar objects — a glass of water or a cake of soap — in his effort to evoke every aspect of them in the verbal web of his poem. He thinks of his poems as a kind of game: he is the man of the "objeu" played with the world. And he explains his activity: "Yes we are working on a new way of thought but no, it is not one prescribed to us by Marx or Hegel. Yes we are working on a renewal of minds, but *not* in what concerns their social relationships (yes, that too) rather in what concerns their relationships with the *mute world*." * His function as poet, as he sees it, is to reach via speech the specifity of each object as it truly impinges on his sensitivity, and it gives him intense enjoyment. He has done away with the existential theme of anguish and calls upon us to play our role confidently as "creators and users of language." One may not like what he does with language but though he is unique in the way he writes he is not unique in his orientation.

What a number of French writers seem to be seek-

* "Ponge and the Poetry of Self-knowledge," Sarah N. Lawall in *Contemporary Literature,* University of Wisconsin Press, Spring, 1970.

ing is to increase our attentiveness to the world around us and thereby, our acuity of perception and our sensitivity to that world; perhaps, as a quite different kind of poet Alain Bosquet suggests, it is because since Hiroshima the poet feels a new responsibility toward our earth, almost a new tenderness when faced by its vulnerability at our hands. And when Ponge rejects the dictates of abstract constructs, he is also indirectly reiterating a theme which is fundamental in our present literature, that is the uncompromising assertion of the writer's need for freedom. As Robbe-Grillet has said of the creator, "the slightest external directive paralyzes him." This acute sensitivity to the menace of outer control is different in kind from the great Romantic rebellion. Writers, who perforce use language, have proved the best allies in our struggle against the assault made upon our freedom, directly or indirectly, through perverted uses of language. Their revolt and apparent crudity — even obscenity — is often connected with their discomfort in that sphere.

These are merely fragmentary examples of some of the positive trends in our literature. They indicate that contemporary literature cannot, despite its many disturbing facets, be dismissed as basically insignificant and destructive. Slowly, as we read our contemporaries, write about them, discuss their works from out of the overwhelming mass of publications, and despite the shock of such public catastrophes as war and the confusion of crises, events, predictions and publicity that crowd in upon us and distract us, the quieter configurations of contemporary literature begin to take shape for us and furnish a deeper, steadier, more sustained accompaniment to our lives.

Let us consider for a moment the case of Beckett. Perhaps no writer has been awarded a Nobel prize for so curious

— yet so pertinent — a reason: "for his writing which — in
new forms for the novel and drama — in the dereliction of
modern man acquires its elevation." Far from asserting or
celebrating the presence of the world, Beckett reduces it
until it has virtually disappeared in darkness and silence. And
he proposes no purpose either for his own activity as writer
or for the human presence in the world. Yet he is read with
passionate interest by a number of people, and a host of studies
have collected around his writing.

In one of his rare press interviews Beckett made a surpris-
ing statement. He never, he declared, reads philosophers and
does not understand them. The key to his writing, he said,
must be sought in his sensibility, for it is there and there alone
that his strange characters and their strange environment are
somehow born. Yet Descartes is the narrator of one of his
poems; he alludes to Democritus and Schopenhauer; and the
Pythagoreans and Guelincx have never ceased to haunt his
world. His novels — especially *Watt* — contain a quasi Rabel-
aisian parody of all the logical and rhetorical devices that have
permitted Western man, like Beckett's own Ubuesque creation, the "man-pot" Mahood, to hold over his skull for protec-
tion a "partially waterproof tarpaulin." Most of us I think
know Wallace Stevens' poem:

> *I placed a jar in Tennessee*
> *And round it was upon a hill*
> *It made the slovenly wilderness*
> *Surround that hill.*

Beckett's "man-jar" is a rather different creation, though it
does oblige us to look again at that strange being, man, to
which we are so accustomed. As the critic Howard Nemerov
remarked of Wallace Stevens' jar, the spell cast over the chaos
by the poet's act is temporary, the formless "wilderness" is

still there. No systems of order in which we find shelter are entirely waterproof in Beckett's view. It was not he, he remarked in the interview, who had created the confusion. It was there, so he had to let it in.

Describing, reasoning, discussing, examining—Beckett's characters never tire of these activities, though no two of them ever proceed in the same way. They share our "deplorable mania" not only to want "when something happens to know what" but furthermore to know why. Beckett is something of a contemporary Faust who through the agency of his characters mimes with ferocious humor and so undermines all our past and present attempts to "think out" our situation, to give it an intelligible structure. Not without reason did he invent Macmann, the character Malone talks to himself about, who while believing that "he had done as any man of goodwill would have done in his place and with very much the same results" nonetheless admits that, in gardening, he is "incapable of weeding a bed of pansies or marigolds and of leaving one standing." The sentence in French turns on a pun: *"pensées"* as both flower and thought. Macmann like Beckett is a gently compulsive iconoclast. Beckett's verbal clowning by indirection and mime produces the same devastation in our own mental flower-beds. His curious inventions —such as his invention of the "man-pot"—allow him to reduce his characters' relations with the physical world to the most schematic: two pots for nourishment and evacuation; a bag of canned foods; a pebble or, in prosperous times, sixteen pebbles to suck. With his particular brand of humor he externalizes in his novels a "mental country," in which everything unfolds in the "imperfect shade" and "doubtful light" which one of Beckett's characters, Malone, calls "my light."

From out of this semi-darkness emerge the Beckettian characters, the "large articulates" whose peculiar forms of articulation in body, thought, and speech make them forget that they are in fact "frightened vagabonds" dying by degrees, while words and image spin around in their bony white skulls. They are strangely intent on travel if only in spirit; and when bedridden or "in jars" they insist on telling the story of their travels. They are all related, each emerging out of another. Identified with each in turn, yet each time re-emerging, modified by the contact. There always finally remains he who is the nameless one, known only by his voice, a voice which is his and not his own — who is "alone here the first and the last" — and nonetheless is never there, the animator of this verbal cosmos. Beckett's characters are all victimized by words, "entrusted with missions," and inhabited by voices. They are sometimes in touch with emissaries who force them to write or to speak and who must be satisfied. They begin to speak calmly and reasonably, intent on accurately observing and reporting events; but they gradually find themselves impelled into difficult obscure zones where other voices mingle with their own, where other characters appear before them; until in *How it is* one of them, Pim-Bem, emits the hypothesis that perhaps a "not-one-of-us" exists whose "anonymous voice" is heard in the blurred but nonetheless communicable words extracted from, murmured by the infinite series of Bem Pim Bom that he glimpses crawling very slowly in the mud in closed ranks from west to east. Meantime the nameless narrator who after *Watt* always begins the story in the first person speaks on and on. He gives us an account of an activity he does not understand and which threatens to overwhelm him. "The voice that speaks knowing that it lies, indifferent to what it says; knowing itself useless . . . not listening to itself but to the silence that it breaks."

To break the silence, to name the unnameable and speak the unspeakable, the narrator must resort to the "jokes," fairy tales and lies that enable his characters to make their way toward the light, in other words, to fiction. The characters he invents all wear the Beckett uniform or what remains thereof, if only the long white hair, dirty and matted by the accumulated filth of centuries.

We soon realize that it is the same adventurer who goes his way from book to book. Beckett is following his own adventure on the trail "of that little creature in numerous disguises who haunts him," man. He too, like his characters, must set out again after each book. Grim, pathetic, funny, his own adventure rejoins the long monotonous human enterprise inscribed in our written language and which obliges us always to take another look at that small mythic figure, man. We find one of his avatars in one of Beckett's essay-poems entitled *Sans* (without, or maybe in a pun, meaning). "Ruins, real refuge at last toward which from so far by so many false. Horizons without end, earth sky mingled. Grey face, two pale blue small body beating heart alone upright." When all is torn away the small human figure still stands a haunting enigmatic presence, confronting the world with a pathetic kind of courage. In the image we sense besides a power of emotion, a truth we recognize and an unspoken respect. All valid literature, even the most satiric, reaches for such forms of respect, respect for people, for things, for truth. Sometimes, when it is new, we have trouble going beyond the form.

It is not easy to define the literary experience. Wallace Fowlie, in a brilliant essay,* states what he sees as the role

---

* "A Stock-taking: French literature in the 1960s," *Contemporary Literature,* Spring, 1970, pp. 137–54.

of art through the centuries. In the Middle Ages, the artist
tried to reconcile man with God; in the neo-classical age, the
artist tried to reconcile man with reason; in the nineteenth
century, with science. In the twentieth century, he suggests,
the artists, the great writers have tried to reconcile man with
himself. I should prefer to say that they have tried to *confront*
man, imaginatively, with himself; and the confrontation has
been cruel sometimes, particularly when writers have felt
that in our time language itself was being debased. It seems
fairly true to say as one of the younger French writers of some
stature, Michel Butor, has said, that literature works at oblig-
ing us to "become contemporary." But not primarily through
its ideological content. Beckett may well be, as a commentator
has claimed, the most qualified spokesman for the atheistic
nihilism of his age, but that is in itself rather unimportant.
What counts in literature is the emotional power of his plays
and novels. His greatness does not lie in the fact that he may
have dramatized the theme of the Hegelian "unhappy conscious" for example. It lies, as Neal Oxenhandler states it[*] in
"his profoundly traditional use of the novel (and stage) as an
emotional matrix where a complex exchange between reader
and novelist takes place," or in the theater between audience
and play. And that is because he involves us emotionally in
the world of his characters, his world. But this, Neal Oxenhandler concludes, "as Beckett himself would say is an argu-
ment for which there is no proof."

   "Don't you see that the whole aim of Newspeak is to
narrow the range of thought? . . . Every year fewer and fewer

---

[*] "Toward the New Aesthetic," *Contemporary Literature,* Spring, 1970, pp.
169–91.

words and the range of thought a little smaller." This is *1984*
and it gives the formula for perfect thought control. The
writer in our time has risen in insurrection against that control. If we then who teach literature make of it the "residence
of forms without force," of formulae, we may miss its essential value which is perhaps not so much to tell us how to live
but to "allow us to breathe" more freely while we live.
Today's literature is consciously breaking with the past and
reflects back to us our anxieties, but also, as I have tried to
show, some of our aspirations. It often puts upon us quite a
burden when we first approach it, transmitting no "message"
but rather a rich network of suggestions. There seems to be
no doubt at all that our consciousness is changing. Our literature does seem to be registering this change. In this very
modest sense it is fulfilling an indispensable function, the
mediation of that change.

SCIENCE AND THE HUMANITIES
IN THE RENAISSANCE

SCIENCE AND THE HUMANITIES
IN THE RENAISSANCE

Louis B. Wright

THOUGHTFUL MEN ARE TROUBLED by the state of learning in the world that we have inherited. Some pessimists gloomily predict a return to the Dark Ages, to a world that will care as little about learning as did Europe before the rise of the monks of Cluny in the tenth century. Learning, others point out, has become so specialized and fractionalized that the humanist can no longer comprehend science and the scientist has no time for humanism. In attempting to imitate the methods of the scientist, the humanist is accused of reducing the humanities to an arid desert without meaning to the generality of men.

Perhaps we might profitably consider for a moment the ideals of humanistic learning in the early Renaissance, when men rediscovered the values of the classical world and attempted to apply them to life in the fifteenth and sixteenth centuries. Our own lives are infinitely more complicated, to be sure, than were the lives of the men of the Renaissance, or at least we think so, but humanistic values of that earlier

[45]

age still have validity for us if we can understand them aright. We particularly need to realize the unity of learning, scientific and humanistic. We cannot live successfully in two worlds. All of us, as best we can, must attempt to comprehend, if not the technicalities, at least the implications of both worlds. Indeed, it is my observation that some scientists are also excellent humanists, and the latter, as did the men of the Renaissance, ought to make more of an effort to comprehend the world of science.

Our world at this particular moment in time is peculiar and puzzling. As parents sometimes say of children, perhaps we are merely going through a "phase," but it is unlike any phase that history has recorded. For the first time, the elders in sophisticated society, the elders of the more educated groups, seem bent upon abandoning their inheritance. With precipitate haste such as the Belgians displayed in leaving the Congo, our sophisticated elders are fleeing responsibility and proclaiming the wisdom and divinity of youth. They give every evidence of bad conscience. Because they have been unable to insure the millennium, they would abandon their mistakes to a younger generation whose ignorance and inexperience are sufficient to give them both arrogance and assurance. Academic sophisticates have been especially eager to cry *peccavi*. Some among us would turn control over to the most virginal minds in the student body. Innocence of knowledge or experience has somehow become a virtue, particularly innocence of any taint of history or antiquity. In this we differ markedly from the Renaissance. And some of our humanists, who are in the forefront of this new dispensation, would be a puzzle to their counterparts in the fifteenth century.

The fifteenth century believed in the wisdom of the ancients. We have proclaimed our freedom from the fetters of antiquity. Our ancestors thought that the accumulated wisdom of the race had certain universal values. We appear to believe that originality and experimentation are the prime values, and that we ought not be handicapped by any encrustations of knowledge from the past. So youth disdains the classics and concentrates upon emanations from the authors who happen to be fashionable at the moment, in the belief that if a writer is contemporary he is also "relevant," one of the most abused and most misunderstood words in the language. Unhappily what is "relevant" at noon today may not be relevant at three p.m. tomorrow. The Renaissance differed from us in this respect because they found intense relevance in classical literature, and they made practical use of the classics in everyday life. I shall provide illustrations of this in a few moments. Although the Renaissance had its share of indecent writing, they did not elevate it to "relevance." Pietro Aretino, for example, wrote bawdy sonnets and dialogues, and men laughed at them, but nobody solemnly found them "significant"; yet some of our critics discover deep truths in *Portnoy's Complaint* and similar writings.

The Renaissance humanists were men of intense purpose, and their purposes were practical. They did not retreat into an ivory tower; they did not consider themselves an anointed priestcraft; they did not invent a special jargon of their trade; they did not write merely for one another; they did not go to conventions of their kind and spend their time in self-congratulation; particularly they did not despise the men of the marketplace and the forum. They sought to communicate to the generality of men, and their communication had a purpose, practical and utilitarian.

In our time, it has been unfashionable to apply the words "practical" and utilitarian" to the sacred subjects of

the humanities. We have subscribed to a perverse view that
the humanities ought to be above and beyond ordinary useful-
ness. Indeed, I am afraid we have sometimes tended to believe
that the humanities were too rarefied and precious for appre-
ciation and understanding by the common herd. More
recently, some of our advanced thinkers in this area would
identify the common herd no longer with the unwashed
(now elevated to sanctity like the desert saints), but with
what *Time* magazine calls "Middle America" — the middle
class. William Shakespeare would be vastly puzzled by the
attitude of certain practitioners of poetry and criticism in our
time. He held extremely bourgeois views. He wanted to make
money. So he wrote with one eye on the box office and car-
pentered his plays to attract the largest possible audience. He
had a supreme sense of the theatre and knew precisely what
would go, on the stage. These qualities did not interfere with
the genius of a great poet and dramatist. Hence his plays have
lived through the changing fashions of the centuries. One
might note in passing that closet drama, drama written in the
study for the delectation of the precious few, has never lived
or exerted much influence in the world.

Many of the greatest scholars, artists, and writers of the
early Renaissance were practical men, convinced that their
efforts should be purposeful and should serve society, though
they did not use that word. They were likely to say that they
served their prince or the state.

Some of these Renaissance figures were also scientists
and engineers. They suffered no delusions about the sacred-
ness of humanistic disciplines. They applied their art to the
problems of the day in as sensible a way as they knew how.
And they took pride in their competence, the variety of their
skills, and the breadth of their knowledge. Narrow specializa-

tion was not for them. They might insist that one or another of their accomplishments transcended the others, but they did not apologize for diverse interests. Michelangelo, for example, constantly denied that he was a painter. When Pope Julius II kept plaguing him to get on with the decoration of the Sistine Chapel, Michelangelo replied in letters always signed "Michelangelo Buonarroti, Sculptor."

In a political emergency, the city of Florence discovered in humanistic learning practical values that any state might envy. Once more she proved that the pen is more powerful than the sword, but it was the pen of writers in Republican Rome. In the year 1399, Giangaleazzo Visconti, Duke of Milan, was besieging Florence. He planned to add the Florentine Republic to the empire that he was trying to weld together in northern Italy. As a republic, Florence was held in suspicion by other city-states ruled by despots, and Florence needed allies. She also needed doctrines that would encourage her own citizens to hold out against the Milanese soldiers. Florentine scholars found the propaganda the city needed in the works of Cicero and Sallust whose ringing defenses of liberty echoed from that earlier republic whence Florence traced her own beginnings. Thanks to Latin propaganda — and the fortunate death of Giangaleazzo on September 3, 1402 — Florence preserved her freedom.

One of the most famous educators of Renaissance Italy — and one of the great educational figures of the world — was Vittorino da Feltre, a humanist whose teachings remain valid to this day. Better than any other figure of the fifteenth century, Vittorino demonstrated the infinite utility of humane learning. A graduate of the University of Padua, he left a professorship there because of the riotous students — a fami-

liar note — and went to Venice where he set up a school of
his own. Learned in mathematics, Latin, and Greek, Vittorino
sought to adapt the past to the uses of the present. He did not
conceive of the scholar as one who had retired to a life of
contemplation. The scholar owed a debt to society, and he paid
it by teaching others to lead useful and active lives. In other
words, Vittorino by precept and example showed that the
scholar was a public-spirited and patriotic citizen, and he
had no patience with the notion that scholarship gave any
man the right to remain aloof from the ordinary obligations of
society. But he did not go to the opposite extreme. He insisted
that the scholar should serve society in accordance with his
special competence and not pretend to competence in areas
where he had none.

In the 1420s, Gianfrancesco Gonzaga, Marquis of Mantua, was looking for a scholar to establish a school where his
own children could be properly educated. Hearing of the
fame of Vittorino's school in Venice, Gonzaga offered him a
post in Mantua. Vittorino was happy at Venice and made hard
terms. But at last he agreed to come to Mantua. "I accept the
post, on this understanding only," he wrote the Marquis,
"that you require from me nothing which shall be in any
way unworthy of either of us; and I will continue to serve you
so long as your own life shall command respect." * Vittorino
remained in Mantua until his death twenty-three years later
in 1446.

The school that he established gained fame throughout
Italy. At his insistence, the Marquis subsidized poor but
talented scholars and permitted him to accept students, whom

-----

* Eugene F. Rice, Jr. (ed.), *Vittorino da Feltre and Other Humanist
Educators*. By William Harrison Woodward (New York, 1963), p. 24.

Vittorino regarded as promising, from other princely houses of Italy. Vittorino believed in strict discipline, and if a young prince proved worthless, out he went. One of his most worthy princelings was Federigo, later Duke of Urbino, who to the end of his days remembered Vittorino as a master deserving infinite respect. To Vittorino's teaching, this most feared of the condottieri owed the inspiration that made him one of the greatest patrons of learning and the arts of his time.

Vittorino was only one of many great humanistic teachers. If time permitted we could tell of others who had the same ideals, men who taught that learning should develop all sides of man's personality, that it should serve some practical purpose, and that the learned man had an obligation to serve the state to the best of his abilities. That did not mean leading a violent crew of wreckers to break the windows of the Marquis of Mantua's palace, for example.

Another great teacher was Guarino de Verona, whose son Battista wrote in 1459 a treatise, *Upon the Method of Teaching and of Reading the Classical Authors*. Both father and son believed that an educated man had to know Latin and Greek, for these two classical tongues opened vast storehouses of learning and wisdom. Battista Guarino quoted Alexander the Great on the value of a worthy teacher: "Thus the instinct of Alexander of Macedon was a sound one which led him to say that, whilst he owed to his father Philip the gift of life, he owed to his tutor Aristotle an equal debt, namely the knowledge how to use it." Emphasizing the necessity of avoiding a wrong choice in a teacher, Battista declared that a teacher should have good manners.* The emphasis on courtesy runs throughout the educational writings of the time.

---

* *Ibid.,* p. 162.

Violence in manners, barbaric behavior, the humanists taught, marked a man as uneducated and unfit to take a place as a counselor to his prince.

Aeneas Sylvius Piccolomini, later Pope Pius II, in a treatise written as a letter to the young King of Bohemia and Hungary in 1450, commended classical philosophy as a source of wisdom for the education of a gentleman — and he insisted that a leader as well as a teacher ought to be a gentleman. "Respect towards women, affection for children and for home; pity for the distressed, justice towards all, self-control in anger, restraint in indulgence, forbearance in success; contentment, courage, duty — these are some of the virtues to which philosophy will lead you," he asserted.* To achieve these virtues, he commended especially the study of all the works of Cicero, among other classical authors. Most important of Cicero's essays, he considered, were the treatises on old age and friendship. An earlier generation in this country looked upon Cicero's *De Senectute* as a source of wisdom which the young were enjoined to read either in the Latin original or in translation. Nowadays, this treatise on the wisdom of the ancients would doubtless be regarded as heretical if any of this generation had ever heard of it.

The Renaissance did not restrict its definition of humanists merely to professional specialists in linguistics and classical letters. They prized diversity of learning and skills, and they included as humanists the great architects and artists who demonstrated their knowledge of classical learning and of the new science then developing. The division of mankind into two worlds, one of science and one of letters in the manner of Sir Charles Snow, would have been unthinkable in this age.

---

* *Ibid.*, pp. 157–158.

One of the greatest of the early Renaissance architects, Filippo Brunelleschi, who completed the Duomo in Florence by erecting the enormous dome that others had thought impossible, made no pretense of being a man of letters, yet he was the intellectual associate of learned men of his time and was by way of being a literary scholar in such spare time as he could find. He learned geometry from the cosmographer and physician, Paolo Toscanelli, who influenced Columbus. Making himself a careful student of Dante, he took part in learned discussions of that poet and of Christian doctrine illustrated in the *Divine Comedy*. According to Giorgio Vasari, Toscanelli was so impressed with Brunelleschi's expositions that "he thought he was listening to a new St. Paul." * Brunelleschi found time for these intellectual activities while he was designing and supervising the erection of the dome of the Duomo, designing the marvelous Pazzi Chapel, and busying himself in other strictly professional duties.

One of the brilliant Renaissance humanists who is not well enough known to English-speaking peoples is Leon Battista Alberti, truly a Renaissance man as we understand that synonym for versatility. Born in Venice in 1404, son of an exiled Florentine, Alberti grew up among artists and intellectuals but he never lost contact with the ordinary man in the street. Indeed, that is one of the characteristics of Renaissance Italians. Steeped in Latin literature, probably taught by the famous Latin humanist, Gasparino da Barzizza at Milan, Alberti early demonstrated his literary ability. When a student at the University of Bologna, he wrote a comic piece in Latin, attributed to an ancient Roman, one Lepidus, whose work Alberti claimed to have discovered in an old manuscript. It

* Giorgio Vasari, *The Lives of the Painters, Sculptors, and Architects* (4 vols., London, 1963), II, 272.

was written so well that it fooled the great printer Aldus Manutius, who published it as a newly-discovered classic. From this time onward, Alberti was recognized for his wit and learning, as well as for his many skills. One of a small group of brilliant spirits whom Lorenzo the Magnificent brought together at a summer resort for conversation, Alberti outshone them all. His writings were numerous and varied: comic pieces of satire, treatises on the art of love, the tranquility of the soul, on the law, on the qualities of his dog, on horse-breeding, amorous verses, and serious treatises on painting, sculpture, architecture, politics, the government of a family, and an Italian grammar. In fact his grammar of the Italian language has been described as "the first modern grammar of a living European language." * And he proved his own abilities in the practice of more than one craft: artist, sculptor, architect, and engineer.

In 1441 we find Alberti in Florence organizing a public contest among poets. As a philosopher, he cast his influence on the side of the active rather than the contemplative life, but the activism of Alberti and the other humanists of his time was constructive rather than destructive. Although these men were aware of the shortcomings of society and the inequities of governments, they did not seek to destroy but to correct and rebuild. The dignity of man could be achieved, Alberti maintained, in work and only in work. Every man should have a calling and labor in it, each according to his abilities, he insisted. This was common doctrine in this period and persisted down to recent times. Only in our time has the virtue of work for its own sake been called into question.

---

* Leon Battista Alberti, *The Family in Renaissance Florence. A Translation by Renée Neu Watkins of I Libri della Famiglia by Leon Battista Alberti* (Columbia, S.C., 1969), p. 7.

Lest we dismiss Alberti as a mere dilettante with time to write a shelf-full of books expounding his views, let us remember that he was the architect of the Tempio Malatestiana in Rimini, of the façade of Santa Maria Novella in Florence, of the Palazzo and logia Ruccelai in Florence, of the churches of San Sebastiano and San Andrea in Mantua, and of many other buildings. His treatise of architecture, *De re aedificatoria*, written in Latin and translated into Italian and many other languages, had a lasting influence. Though Alberti went back to the Roman architect Vitruvius for inspiration, he based many of his observations on actual measurements that he himself had made among the surviving classical structures in Rome.

Few men of his time better illustrated the union of both the active and the contemplative life than Alberti, but obviously the active, the constructively active, predominated. Alberti bore his share of a citizen's responsibility. Vasari praised him for uniting theory and practice: "But when theory and practice are united in one person, the ideal condition is attained, because art is enriched and perfected by knowledge, the opinions and writings of learned artists having more weight and more credit than the words or works of those who have nothing more to recommend them beyond what they have produced, whether it be done well or ill. The truth of these remarks is illustrated by Leon Battista Alberti, who, having studied the Latin tongue and practiced architecture, perspective, and painting, has left works to which modern artists can add nothing, although numbers of them have surpassed him in practical skill." *

---

* Vasari, *Lives,* I, 346.

Devotion to the humanities and a recognition of their value to society were not confined to professional scholars or to brilliant geniuses like Leon Battista Alberti. Few more devoted humanists could be found in all Italy than Federigo da Montefeltro, Duke of Urbino, who lived between the years 1422 and 1482. Most famous of the condottieri, those professional soldiers who sold their services to the highest bidders, Federigo was also a learned man, a patron of artists and writers, who made the court of Urbino virtually an academy. His fame as a soldier was so great that Venice once paid him 80,000 ducats just to stay at home when Venice was waging war against Ferrara. His love of books was so great that he employed the leading bookman of the age, Vespasiano da Bisticci, as his collector and had between thirty and forty copyists duplicating manuscripts for his library, for he would not tolerate a printed book among these works, beautifully bound in crimson and silver. His books eventually went to the Vatican Library. Federigo employed five men whose duty it was to read aloud to him at meals. Learned in Latin literature himself, he never forgot the teachings of his master, Vittorino da Feltre. He even had his portrait painted in full armor, reading a book. To his son Guidobaldo he passed on his love of letters, and it was Guidobaldo's court that Baldassare Castiglione described in *Il Cortegiano,* translated into English by Sir Thomas Hoby in 1561 as *The Book of the Courtier.* Few books of the Renaissance had such a civilizing influence as Castiglione's and did so much to transmit humanistic ideals. Some of the early settlers of colonial America brought *The Book of the Courtier* with them so that they might have the best guide to conduct becoming a gentleman.

Federigo da Montefeltro was an eminently practical man, himself interested in science and engineering as well as the humanities. His scientific study of artillery — and the application of his learning in this field — made him the foremost soldier of his generation. The mathematics Federigo learned from Vittorino, along with his Latin and Greek, made the artillery of Urbino feared and envied throughout Italy. Federigo could see no divorce between science and the humanities. In his concept, and in that of learned men of his time, the two went together.

The best-remembered genius of the Renaissance, of course, is Leonardo da Vinci, whose diversity of intellectual interests has excited wonder from his own time to ours. Though Leonardo's qualities are well known, we can well afford to devote a few moments to the contemplation of the vast range of this man's learning and the way he applied his learning to practical problems. The painter of the Mona Lisa thought of himself less as an artist than as an engineer, an experimental scientist, and a research student. His research in anatomy, for example, was so thorough and discerning that medical historians devote almost as much space to Leonardo's discoveries in human anatomy as they do to those of Vesalius.

Painter, sculptor, writer, architect, physicist, botanist, geologist, paleontologist, zoologist, anatomist, and engineer, Leonardo placed art last on his list of accomplishments. When writing to Lodovico Sforza, Duke of Milan, to seek employment, he placed engineering first among his qualifications, and became Lodovico's military engineer. He built fortresses, dams, and canals. An artilleryman at heart, he improved the rapidity of fire by inventing a breech-loading cannon and a prototype of the machine gun. When Milan fell to the French in 1499 — in spite of Leonardo's engineering — he returned to Florence and in 1502 took service with Cesare Borgia who named him his "engineer-general." Incidentally, Leonardo, like Machiavelli, admired Cesare Borgia because he believed that Borgia had the strength and ability to unite the warring city-states of Italy and weld them into a nation. Unfortunately, Borgia disappointed his admirers and fell a victim to his own wickedness.

Leonardo was a very modern man, indeed, and turned his talents to town planning and the problems of pollution. For the Duke of Urbino he drew up a plan for sewage disposal. We do not often think of the painter of the Last Supper on the walls of the refectory of Santa Maria delle Grazie as an engineer busy with the layouts of sewer systems. After an outbreak of the plague in Milan, he recommended to Lodovico Sforza a program for population dispersal into satellite towns.

For Florence, plagued with floods, he recommended a canal to divert the waters of the Arno into a freight-carrying waterway to the sea. To overcome the problems of the hilly terrain between Florence and the Mediterranean, he proposed to tunnel the hills, and he devised boring tools for the purpose. Unfortunately the Florentine authorities, deciding the cost would be too great, left the Arno uncurbed. If Leonardo's advice had been taken, Florence might have been spared the flood that we so vividly remember.

During the last phase of his life, when Leonardo was the guest of King Francis I of France and lived at Cloux, we will be in error if we think of the artist sitting before an easel painting. Actually, he was busy with his own research and with practical problems: architectural designs and his royal patron's pet projects for canals. Leonardo was a great artist and a great humanist, but he applied his learning and his art to practical problems of the world around him. Into his notebooks he once wrote, "Thou, O God, dost sell unto us all good things at the price of labor," and again he noted this sentiment: "Shun those studies in which the work that results dies with the worker." * Here was a humanist who thought constructively. If society in Leonardo's time was imperfect, he at least would do his part to improve it rather than tear it down.

Only a little less behind Leonardo in versatility was Michelangelo, sculptor, painter, architect, and poet. Always a modest man, Michelangelo stoutly denied that he was a painter. On more than one occasion he wrote, "I am no painter." Yet this was the artist who spent four long years painting the magnificent frescoes of the Sistine Chapel that today are the wonder of the world.

After the sack of Rome in 1527 by the troops of the Emperor Charles V, Michelangelo was employed by Florence as military engineer to fortify the hill of San Miniato. The sculptor of the David did an equally superb job of building forts on the hill overlooking Florence.

Like Leonardo, Michelangelo studied anatomy from dissections, and he told Vasari that he regretted that he could not write a treatise upon the subject, but modesty about his skill of expression prevented. Vasari remarks, however, that Michelangelo always "clearly expressed his ideas in a few words," certainly a virtue in a prolix age. "He was very fond of reading the Italian poets," Vasari continued, "especially Dante, whom he much admired and whose ideas he adopted. Petrarch was also a favorite author of his, and he delighted in composing serious madrigals and sonnets upon which commentaries have since been made." He mentions a lecture on

* William B. Parsons, *Engineers and Engineering in the Renaissance* (Baltimore, 1939), p. 22.

one of Michelangelo's sonnets delivered before the Florentine Academy and the poetic exchanges between Michelangelo and his great friend Vittoria Colonna, Marchesa of Pescara.

Michelangelo had a satirical sense of humor which his contemporaries did not always appreciate. In painting the Last Judgment in the Sistine Chapel, he inserted the portrait of a pompous Papal official as a devil in Hell. When the official complained to Pope Paul III and demanded that he be removed from his undignified pose, the Pope smiled and replied that if Michelangelo had pictured him in Purgatory he might have intervened, but the Pope had no jurisdiction over Hell.

Michelangelo, again like Leonardo, had a bourgeois respect for money and saw to it that he was well paid for his services. But he was exceedingly generous and gave away thousands of ducats to deserving friends. Most of the great artists saw to it that they were well-paid. An exception to the rule was Donatello, who was so careless of money that he kept his cash in a basket suspended by a cord from the ceiling of his studio. Cosimo de' Medici, concerned about Donatello's carelessness, left instructions in his will that his executors were to see that the improvident sculptor did not suffer.

As a poet, Michelangelo enjoyed a contemporary reputation that placed him in the first rank as a man of letters. But he was invariably modest about his literary accomplishments. In his old age he sent a sonnet to Vasari that tells of his melancholy:

> Arrived already is my life's brief course,
> Through a most stormy sea, in a frail bark,
> At mankind's common port and at the shores
> Where one accounts for one's deeds, bright or dark.

O now I know how foolish and how stark
My art has been, so far from its true source,
And how I made an idol and a monarch
Of something that, alas, gives but remorse.

Of all my thoughts of love, once gay and light,
What will now be, if two deaths I'm near?
Of the first I am sure, the second I dread.
Painting no more, nor sculpture, can now quiet
My soul, turned to that Love divine that, here,
*To take us, opened its arms on a cross and bled.**

Michelangelo combined those traits of humanism that
the philosophers so often discussed, the contemplative and
the active life. Although he loved solitude, he never withdrew
from the world or retired within himself. He participated in
the affairs of his time, spending his last years in the active
supervision of the rebuilding of St. Peter's in Rome. He spent
his strength and his eyesight painting the ceiling of the Sistine Chapel, and he could build effective forts on San Miniato
to protect Florence. In the meantime he could write moving
sonnets to Vittoria Colonna. Here was a humanist who
achieved supreme greatness and never let arrogance spoil his
sense of values.

Among the learned humanists of the fifteenth and early
sixteenth centuries were several distinguished physicians. One
of these was an Englishman, Thomas Linacre, who received
his medical degree at Padua and spent several years in Italy

---

* *The Complete Poems of Michelangelo. Translated into Verse with Notes
and Introduction by Joseph Tusiani* (London, 1960), pp. 151–152.

absorbing the new learning, especially Greek. In Florence he was welcomed by Lorenzo the Magnificent and permitted to share with two Medici princes instruction in Greek. One of the young Medici, Giovanni, later became Pope Leo X. Linacre carried back to England an enthusiasm for Greek and Latin learning; for the rest of his life he pursued a career as physician to Henry VII and Henry VIII, and combined the practice of medicine with the teaching of Greek. Thomas More learned his Greek from Linacre, and Erasmus, when he came to England, sat at his feet. Linacre also wrote in two fields, and achieved a reputation for learning from both his grammatical and his medical works. Thomas Fuller called him the "restorer of learning," and others have believed that Browning had Linacre in mind when he wrote "The Grammarian's Funeral." * His translations of Galen's medical treatises from Greek into Latin gave European physicians the most accurate versions of the Greek physician's work they had yet possessed.

Among the Renaissance medical humanists, we ought to remember François Rabelais, who satirized pedantry but was himself a man of vast learning and the translator of Hippocrates' aphorisms into Latin.

Still another important medical humanist of the Renaissance was Girolamo Fracastoro of Verona — physician, physicist, astronomer, geologist, and poet. He recognized the significance of fossils, was probably the first scientist to discuss the magnetic poles, and chose Latin poetry as the means of discussing the diagnosis and treatment of syphilis. Few other physicians have grown lyrical to this extent in writing tech-

---

* Fielding H. Garrison, *An Introduction to the History of Medicine* (Philadelphia and London, 1960), p. 195.

nical papers. Fracastoro's *Syphilis sive Morbus Gallicus,* published in Venice in 1530, gave the name by which this disease has since been known. Fracastoro, usually Latinized to Fracastorius, was a genius in advance of his time, a humanist of vast learning, and a physician with discriminating insights; for example, he suspected that infections were caused by microorganisms.*

The tradition of humanist-physicians has extended from the Renaissance to our own time. The Johns Hopkins University — and the Tudor and Stuart Club founded by Sir William Osler — have included many excellent humanists among its distinguished physicians. Despite the tremendous burden of keeping up with their own professional literature, medical doctors have frequently been men of letters.

The humanistic philosophers of the Renaissance gave a great impetus to scientific research when they emphasized the omnipresence of God in Nature. Pico della Mirandola, disciple of Marsilio Ficino, the great Platonist, helped to reconcile Christianity and Platonism and to popularize the idea of the goodness of the universe. Ficino, one might note, was also a physician. Since God's world was good, men had a moral right, even an obligation, to study the beneficence of the Creator in providing man with so much that was both good and desirable. With such justification, investigators turned to examine the physical world around them, and the spirit of scientific research was born.

If the Italian humanists needed encouragement for their ideal of versatility, they received it from the example of Lorenzo de' Medici, called "the Magnificent." The head of a great international banking house, the leader of the oligarchy

---

* *Ibid.,* pp. 232–233.

that really ruled Florence, Lorenzo had time to be a poet and
a student of the classics. He also concerned himself with such
practical matters as the improvement of dairy cattle, the development of a botanical garden, and the breeding of race horses.
An architect himself of no mean ability, he submitted a design
for the completion of the cathedral of Florence in competition
with some of the greatest artists and architects of the day. A
profound student of the classics, Lorenzo was the patron of
scholars and the encourager of learning.* By precept and
example, he emphasized the value of the humanities to society.

We could spend vastly more time than the duration of
patience of a lecturer's audience enumerating the qualities
of a multitude of humanists who shared Lorenzo's views about
the obligations of the scholar to serve society. That, indeed,
has been the goal of all great humanists from the Renaissance
to our own time. We should not forget that many scholars in
fields of the humanities have made great contributions to the
well-being of mankind in the twentieth century. Neither
should we forget that many scientists are also humanists in
their points of view and often in their attainments. Too much
has been made of the separation of these two great areas
of learning.

Too often in recent years, some of those who lay claim
to being humanists have fallen short of their high calling and
become either cynical or iconoclastic. Some have withdrawn
from the world of reality and devoted themselves to the cul-
tivation of a self-destroying guild, a kind of occult priestcraft
in which they talk only to one another and write only for the
understanding of the anointed. A few have even become

---

* See Vincent Cronin, *The Florentine Renaissance* (New York, 1967),
pp. 216–217.

leaders of the cult of destruction and have proclaimed a revolution, but a curious revolution that has no positive aims, merely the destruction of society as it exists.

An article by Kenneth Eble entitled "The Scholarly Life" in the winter issue of *American Scholar* (1969) concludes with an indictment of contemporary humanistic scholarship and its advocates. The author asserts:

The shame of humanistic study in the face of so much that needs to be done is the vast amount of learning that means little to the person doing it, little to the scholar supervising it, and nothing whatsoever to the society that supports it. Part of the scholar's task must be that of removing some of the undergrowth that scholarship has encouraged to grow up around formal study in the humanities. Another part is to make humanistic scholarship generous to attract more of the intelligence, imagination, and energy of young scholars.*

Professor Eble's indictment may be too severe, but all of us who have watched the progress of humanistic scholarship and so-called "research" during the two decades past know that an enormous amount of these pursuits have no meaning and no purpose. The lack of a sense of values among the practitioners of the humanities is one of the serious problems facing the humanistic disciplines today. A scholar need not become an "activist" in the current meaning of the term — that is a banner-carrier ready to "demonstrate" at the twitch of a whisker about matters of which he has little real knowledge. Too often that is the extent of the present-day humanist's

---

*Kenneth Eble, "The Scholarly Life," *The American Scholar* XXXIX (Winter, 1969–70), pp. 109–122.

participation in the problems of society. But the humanists might study the role of the Renaissance humanists to see how they applied their learning in areas where they knew they could make a contribution.

A critic will at once object that no longer can a man of letters be also an artist, an architect, or a physician as could humanists in the Renaissance. Our world of learning has become too complex for such participation. But the humanistic scholar can still apply his abilities systematically to problems of education, the advancement of genuine learning, politics, and social welfare.

The student of the humanities has an opportunity to be conversant with the best that has been thought and said in the past. His discipline brings him into intimate contact with great minds, and his studies ought to induce a sense of perspective, proportion, and discrimination. For centuries men have believed that humanistic disciplines are useful in the training of leaders. Thomas Jefferson pointed out that republics are liable to fall when their supply of leaders of intelligence and character fails. He believed that a democratic society should make provisions for liberal studies to insure an adequate succession of leaders. Many generations before Jefferson, Rabelais also commended liberal studies as necessary to a well-ordered state, and he warned against those scholars who took refuge in nooks and crannies that kept them away from a full and active life. Men should not grow squint-minded, he declared, nor look out at life through a little hole.

If the professors of liberal studies do not make the most of their opportunities, if they cultivate only a small priestcraft, they will grow squint-minded. Today we need humanists who have wisdom acquired from a profound study of the best thought that has gone before, humanists who are concerned with distilling the wisdom of the ancients and transmitting it to potential leaders. As Vittorino long ago maintained, such teachers ought to be men whose example would induce worthy emulation, men who would emphasize the importance of character no less than learning. The humanist today has a vital role to play, and he would do well to contemplate the ideals and the practice of the great minds of the Renaissance.

At the end of World War I, Sir William Osler, a great teacher of medicine and a man of liberal studies himself, surveyed the state of learning in an essay, *The Old Humanities and the New Science* (Boston, 1920) and prescribed the study of the classics for the disease of specialism that he saw overtaking education, scholarship, and science itself. In a footnote he quoted with approval the platform for a liberal education recommended by Professor J. A. Stewart of Oxford: "No humane letters without natural science, and no natural science without humane letters." Society as a whole requires this fusion of the most significant branches of learning. Both humanists and scientists must struggle toward this end, difficult as it may be in an era of increasing complexity.